Inventions and Discoveries

Mathematics

WORLD
BOOK

a Scott Fetzer company

Chicago

www.worldbookonline.com

World Book, Inc.
233 N. Michigan Avenue
Chicago, IL 60601
U.S.A.

For information about other World Book publications, visit our Web site at **http://www.worldbookonline.com** or call **1-800-WORLDBK (967-5325).**
For information about sales to schools and libraries, call **1-800-975-3250 (United States),** or **1-800-837-5365 (Canada).**

Editorial:
Editor in Chief: Paul A. Kobasa
Project Manager: Cassie Mayer
Editor: Daniel Kenis
Content Development: Odyssey Books
Writer: Cheryl Reifsnyder
Researcher: Cheryl Graham
Manager, Contracts & Compliance
  (Rights & Permissions): Loranne K. Shields
Indexer: David Pofelski

Graphics and Design:
Manager: Tom Evans
Coordinator, Design Development and Production:
  Brenda B. Tropinski
Contributing Designer: Adam Weiskind
Photographs Editor: Kathy Creech

Pre-Press and Manufacturing:
Director: Carma Fazio
Manufacturing Manager: Steven K. Hueppchen
Production/Technology Manager: Anne Fritzinger

Picture Acknowledgments:
Front Cover: © moodboard/SuperStock.
Back Cover: © Mary Evans Picture Library/Alamy Images.

© Classic Image/Alamy Images 33; © Mark Gabrenya, Alamy Images 34; © Juniors Bildarchiv/Alamy Images 23; © ton koene, Alamy Images 22; © Mary Evans Picture Library/Alamy Images 19, 30, 38; © North Wind Picture Archives/Alamy Images 29, 35; © The Print Collector/Alamy Images 28, 40; © Helene Rogers, Alamy Images 7; © Steve Skjold, Alamy Images 22; © Michael Ventura, Alamy Images 10; Apple Inc. 41; © Bildarchiv Preussischer Kulturbesitz/Art Resource 25; Electron Microscopy Unit, ARS, USDA 16, 44; © Bridgeman Art Library/Getty Images 37; © Hulton Archive/Getty Images 15, 24; © Mark Joseph, Digital Vision/Getty Images 37; © Roger Viollet/Getty Images 21; © John Russell, Photonica/Getty Images 17; © Time & Life Pictures/Getty Images 28, 41, 43; Granger Collection 4; © Mario Villafuerte, Bloomberg News/Landov 42; © Masterfile 32; © David Mendelsohn, Masterfile 5; Shutterstock 5, 7, 9, 10, 11, 12, 13, 16, 20, 21, 26, 30-31, 32, 35, 36, 43, 44; The Louvre, Paris (WORLD BOOK photo by Hubert Josse) 12-13, 44.

All maps and illustrations are the exclusive property of World Book, Inc.

Library of Congress Cataloging-in-Publication Data

Mathematics.
    p. cm. -- (Inventions and discoveries)
  Includes index.
  Summary: "An exploration of the transformative impact of inventions and discoveries in mathematics. Features include fact boxes, sidebars, biographies, timeline, glossary, list of recommended reading and Web sites, and index"--Provided by publisher.
  ISBN 978-0-7166-0391-7
  1. Mathematics--Study and teaching (Secondary)--Juvenile literature.
I. World Book, Inc.
QA135.6.M376 2009
510--dc22
                          2008042561

Inventions and Discoveries
Set ISBN: 978-0-7166-0380-1

Printed in China by:
Shenzhen Donnelley Printing Co., Ltd,
Guangdong Province
2nd Printing February 2010

▶ Table of Contents

There is a glossary of terms on pages 45-46. Terms defined in the glossary are in type **that looks like this** on their first appearance on any spread (two facing pages).

In ancient times, people invented many tools and theories that still help with our understanding of mathematics and the sciences.

What is an invention?

An invention is a new device, new product, or new way of doing something. Inventions change the way people live. Before the car was invented, some people rode horses to travel long distances. Before the light bulb was invented, people used candles and similar sources of light to see at night. Almost 2 million years ago, the invention of the spear and the bow and arrow helped people hunt better. Later, the invention of farming methods allowed people to stay in one place instead of wandering in search of food. Today, inventions continue to change the way people live.

What is mathematics?

Mathematics is the study of numbers, measurements, and space. It was one of the first sciences to develop and is one of the most useful kinds of knowledge. The term *mathematics* comes from a Greek word meaning "inclined to learn."

There are many branches (kinds) of mathematics. Numbers and shapes are the subject of some branches of mathematics. Others help people solve unknown quantities (amounts). Still others help people solve problems involving motion or changing quantities.

People use mathematics every day. Reading a clock, cooking, gardening, and driving are all activities that involve math. Many professions, such as accounting, banking, computer programming, and **engineering,** require strong math skills.

Mathematics is especially impor-

tant in science. In some ways, math is like the language of science, because it allows scientists to communicate facts and ideas exactly. Scientists use math to perform experiments and to test their ideas. All of our modern world's technology and inventions depend on mathematics.

The field of mathematics has a long history of inventions. Some of these inventions are objects you can hold in your hands, such as tools for counting and measuring. Other inventions were ways of writing or thinking about ideas. Even the **symbols** we use to write numbers—0, 1, 2, 3, 4, 5, 6, 7, 8, and 9—are kinds of inventions.

Mathematics has grown and changed throughout history. People have discovered new ways to describe patterns in numbers or shapes. Some of these concepts are used by people in everyday tasks, while others are used only by professional mathematicians to work out complex mathematical problems.

Professional mathematicians study complex mathematical problems and theories.

Scientists use mathematics almost like a language to describe their work.

The Abacus

Counting was important for trade. Ancient people used the abacus to help them count their possessions.

It is hard to imagine a world without numbers. But for much of early human history, the words for numbers did not exist. A number is a **symbol**—that is, an idea that stands for something else. At first, people did not have symbols for numbers. They counted by using objects, such as sticks, pebbles, or the fingers on their hands.

By about 3000 B.C., ancient Egyptians figured out a way to make counting easier. They began using objects that stood for groups of 10 things. For example, a single stone might represent 10 sheep. This made counting large numbers of things easier. Instead of using 100 pebbles to represent 100 sheep, a person could simply use 10 stones, each one worth 10 sheep.

Around the same time that the Egyptians began counting in groups of 10, the Babylonians, who lived in what is now southeastern Iraq, developed a counting system using groups of 60. This way of counting is still in use today. For example, we divide an hour into 60 minutes and each minute into 60 seconds.

Ancient people put objects on tables or boards to count them. Eventually, people in Asia invented a device called an **abacus,** which made counting objects much easier. An abacus is a frame that holds several wires or rods. The rods are strung with beads, which represent numbers.

A typical Chinese abacus has columns of beads separated by a crossbar. Each column has two beads above the crossbar, which each stand for five **units.** Beads below the crossbar stand for one unit.

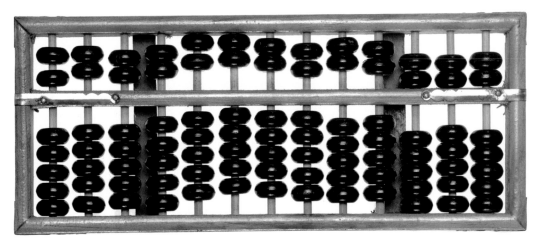

The beads of an abacus are worth different amounts, based on their positions.

The first column on the right of the abacus is the ones column. Each bead below the crossbar has a **value** of one, and each bead above the crossbar represents five units of one, or 5. The second column is the tens column. Each lower bead in the tens column represents one unit of 10, and each upper bead represents five units of 10, or 50. The third column is the hundreds columns, and so on.

By moving the beads on the wires, people could quickly represent many different numbers.

A **CLOSER LOOK**

Ancient people counted in many different ways. In western Africa, people counted using seashells. In South America, the Inca counted by moving kernels of wheat on a board. The ancient Chinese and Japanese moved small sticks on a board. The board was marked with columns for ones, tens, and so on, similar to the idea of an abacus.

▶ Numerals

The invention of the **abacus** helped ancient people count large groups of things, but they still did not have a way to write down these numbers. About 3000 B.C., people in ancient Egypt invented **numerals.** A numeral is a **symbol** that stands for numbers. For example, we use the symbol "20" to represent the number "twenty." Many of the earliest number systems were based on groups of 10.

The ancient Egyptians had different symbols for different groups of numbers. For numbers 1 through 9, they made marks that looked like pictures of fingers. For the number 10, they drew a symbol that looked like an arch. For 100, they drew a coiled rope.

The Egyptians had special symbols for large numbers. For the number 1,000, they drew a symbol that looked like a lotus flower, a type of water lily. Many historians believe that Egyptians chose the lotus flower to stand for 1,000 because it grew in large numbers in Egypt. For the number 100,000, the Egyptians drew a picture of a tadpole. Countless frogs lived along the Nile River in Egypt, which would fill with tadpoles when the frogs' eggs hatched. Some believe that this may be why the Egyptians chose tadpoles for such a large number.

Ancient Egyptians used symbols, called numerals, to stand for certain amounts.

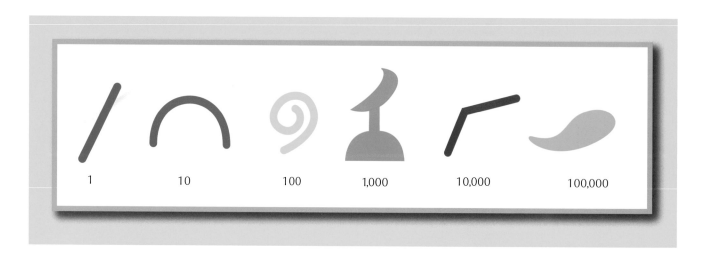

| 1 | 10 | 100 | 1,000 | 10,000 | 100,000 |

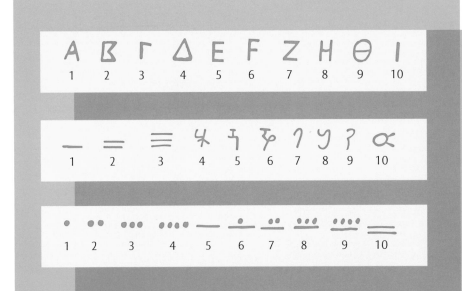

The Greeks used numerals based on their alphabet.

Hindu numerals resemble the ones we use today.

The Maya Indians used lines and dots to write numerals.

At around the same time that the Egyptians developed their own numerals, the Babylonians created number symbols that looked like arrowheads, with each arrowhead representing one **unit.** They drew these symbols on clay tablets.

About 2,500 years later, the ancient Greeks created numbers based on their alphabet. The Hindus in India created numerals that may look very familiar. In fact, their numerals eventually became the ones we use today.

A CLOSER LOOK

Around 500 B.C., the ancient **Romans** created a numeral system that we still use today. Ancient Rome was an empire (group of nations) that reached the height of its power between the A.D. 100's and 200's. The Roman numeral system includes symbols that look like letters from the Roman alphabet. For example, the number 1 looks like the letter I. The number 5 looks like the letter V, and the number 10 looks like the letter X.

The Roman numeral system is still used on the faces of some clocks. It is also used in place of numbers in written texts about people and events in history. For example, "Richard the Third" is often written as "Richard III," and World War One is often written as "World War I."

▶ Fractions

People use fractions when they measure ingredients for baking.

Ancient people created **numerals** to represent amounts of things. But at first, they did not have a way to represent **fractions.** Fractions are parts that make up a whole. For example, if you divided a birthday cake into 12 equal pieces, each piece would equal $^1/_{12}$ of the cake.

More than 4,000 years ago, ancient Babylonian astronomers used fractions by dividing a **unit** into 60 parts. Then they divided each of these units into 60 parts, and so on. This system is still used for telling time in minutes and seconds and for measuring **angles.** People today divide a circle into 360 **degrees** (small measurements). The number 360 is six groups of 60. Other ancient peoples, including Chinese and Egyptians, invented their own way of writing fractions.

About 2,000 years ago, the ancient Greeks wrote fractions with the **numerator** (the number above the line in a fraction) on the bottom and the **denominator** (the number below the line in a fraction) on the top. They did not separate the numerator and denominator by a line. Later, they wrote fractions with the numerator on the top and the de-

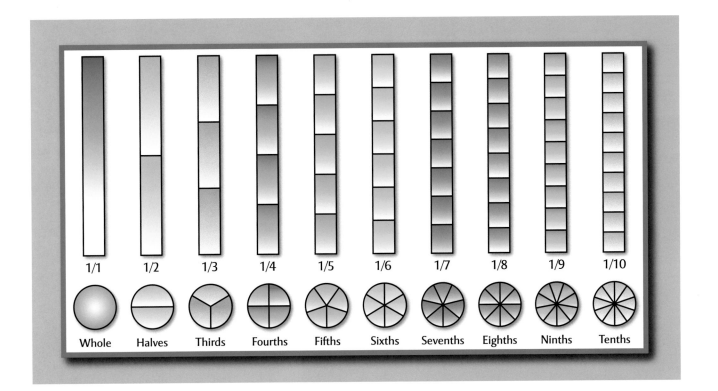

| 1/1 | 1/2 | 1/3 | 1/4 | 1/5 | 1/6 | 1/7 | 1/8 | 1/9 | 1/10 |

| Whole | Halves | Thirds | Fourths | Fifths | Sixths | Sevenths | Eighths | Ninths | Tenths |

nominator on the bottom. Hindu mathematicians in India adopted this method of writing fractions from the ancient Greeks.

During the A.D. 700's, Arabs conquered parts of India. There, they learned the **decimal system** and its method of writing fractions. (See Decimal System, pages 26-27.) The Arabs spread this knowledge through western Asia, across northern Africa, and into Spain.

Fractions allow people to express amounts that are less than a whole.

A CLOSER LOOK

Many problems that were once done with fractions using paper and pencil are now solved with **electronic calculators**, which express fractions in the decimal form. For example, "one-fourth" equals 0.25 in decimal form. However, the fraction form remains important in several areas of mathematics.

► Units of Length

The measuring tools we use today are not too different from ancient measuring tools, such as the cubit.

Today, nearly every home or classroom has a ruler or measuring tape. These simple tools make it much easier to measure the distance between two points. But in prehistoric times, people did not have such tools, so they often used body parts, like their arms, hands, and feet, to measure distance. However, this system was not very accurate, since no two people are the exact same size.

At some point, several early **civilizations** developed a standard measure of length called a **cubit.** The cubit was based on the length of a person's arm from the tip of the middle finger to the elbow.

In ancient Egypt, one cubit was about 20.6 inches (52.3 centimeters) long. The Egyptians divided the cubit into smaller **units** called digits and palms, which related to the parts of a hand. One digit was about the width of a finger. One palm equaled about four digits.

The Egyptians made a bar of granite, a kind of rock, that measured the exact same length as their cubit. They copied this measurement onto sticks, which people could use to measure things. They even used the cubit when making measurements to build the Pyramids of Giza.

In some parts of the world, local

The Egyptian cubit was copied onto sticks so everyone could use it as a standard of measurement.

The ancient Egyptians developed ways to make accurate measurements when they built the pyramids.

leaders established a particular stick of wood or a certain rod of metal as a standard of measurement. They made copies of this standard so they could use it for trade. They placed the original standard in a temple or some other secure place.

Today, people around the world can use the **metric system** as an international standard of measurement. The metric system includes measurements for length, weight, and volume. (See pages 38-39.)

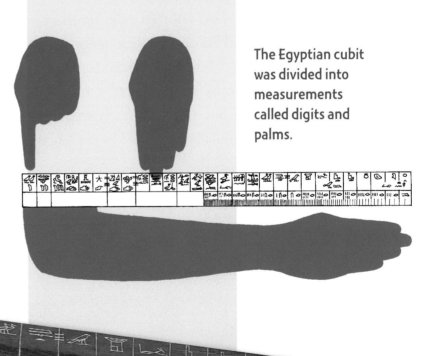

The Egyptian cubit was divided into measurements called digits and palms.

The Pythagorean Theorem

Simple tasks today were extremely difficult thousands of years ago without our modern knowledge of mathematics. For example, it may seem easy to make a field with perfectly square corners, but how could you do this without using modern tools? The ancient Egyptians used math to solve this problem.

Around 2000 B.C., the Egyptians figured out how to use a "magic 3-4-5" triangle to make square corners. They took a rope and tied knots along it, dividing it into 12 equal parts. Each part could be measured by the length between the knots. Then they stretched the rope around three stakes, forming a triangle. They moved the stakes so the sides of this triangle measured 3, 4, and 5 parts of the rope.

In this kind of triangle, the **angle** across from the longest side is perfectly square. A square angle is also called a **right angle.** The 3-4-5 triangle is an example of a right triangle—that is, a triangle that has one right angle. The Egyptians found they could use the 3-4-5 triangle to make square corners.

In the early 400's B.C., students of

A rope with 12 knots wraps around 3 posts to make a 3-4-5 triangle.

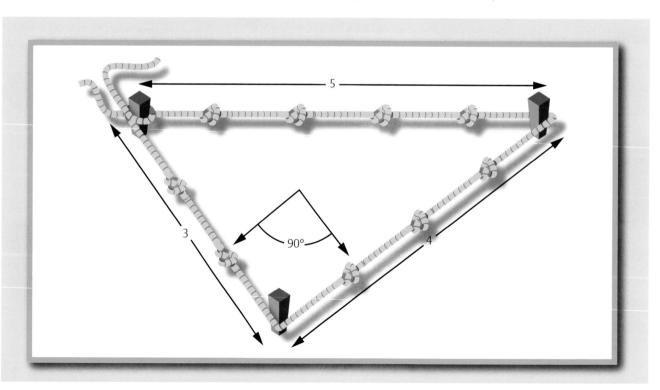

Pythagoras

Pythagoras (580?-? B.C.) was a Greek philosopher and mathematician. Pythagoras believed that numbers were the foundation for everything. For example, he said that colors and virtues were connected to numbers. He also believed that Earth was shaped like a sphere. His followers later taught that Earth moved around a central fire. At the time, most people thought that Earth never moved, and that the sun moved around Earth.

a Greek philosopher named Pythagoras (*pih THAG uhr uhs*) studied the 3-4-5 triangle. These so-called "Pythagoreans" viewed the sides of the triangle as the sides of three squares.

The Pythagoreans knew that a square's **area** (space inside) equals the length of one of its sides, multiplied by itself. For example, the area of the square along the "5" side of a 3-4-5 triangle is 5 x 5, or 25. Using this knowledge, the Pythagoreans discovered that the area of the largest square along the longest side of the 3-4-5 triangle is the same as the areas of the two smaller squares added together.

Let's look at the 3-4-5 triangle shown on this page as an example. To find the area of the square along the longest side, you would multiply 5 x 5 and get 25. To find the area of the

squares along the 3 and 4 sides, you would multiply 3 x 3 (= 9) and 4 x 4 (= 16). Add the area of the two smallest squares together, and you get 9 + 16, which equals 25. This number equals the area of the largest square.

This rule came to be known as the **Pythagorean theorem.** It gave mathematicians a new way to think about numbers, shapes, and relationships between numbers and shapes.

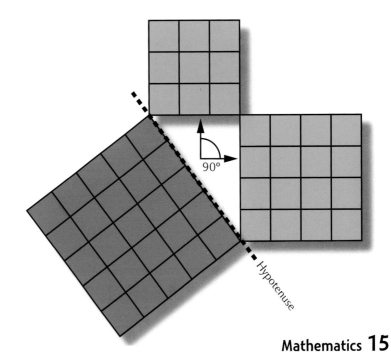

▶ Geometry

Many geometric patterns occur in nature, such as in the shapes of shells and snowflakes.

The ancient Greeks had some of the most advanced mathematicians of any ancient culture. They were the first people to think about and use math in more than purely practical ways. In fact, they were the first to develop many new ideas in an area of mathematics called **geometry.**

Geometry involves the study of shapes, lines, **angles,** and curves. The word *geometry* comes from two Greek words that mean "Earth" and "to measure." People have long been interested in geometric patterns in nature. For example, the shapes of honeycombs, fruits, spiral seashells, and even Earth all relate to geometry.

A Greek mathematician named Euclid (*YOO klihd*) is often called the "father of geometry." Around 300 B.C., Euclid put together a mathematics textbook called *Elements.* The book is one of the most important

FUN FACT

At one point in his life, Euclid taught mathematics in the Egyptian city of Alexandria. According to one story, the Egyptian pharaoh (king) asked Euclid if there was a shorter or easier way to study geometry than his book, *Elements.* Euclid replied, *"There is no royal road to geometry."*

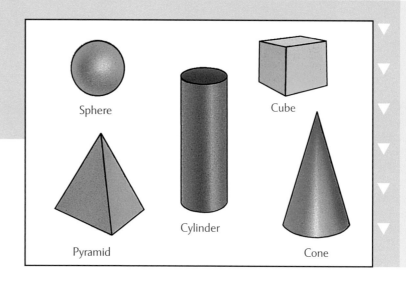

Sphere

Cube

Pyramid

Cylinder

Cone

mathematical works ever. Many of Euclid's ideas in *Elements* are still in use today.

Euclid collected a list of mathematical truths called **axioms.** An axiom is a statement that is assumed to be true, because it is obvious. Here is an example of an axiom: "If there are two different points, there must be a line that goes through both of them." This statement is an axiom because it is obviously true. If you draw two points on a piece of paper, you can always draw a straight line that goes through both of them.

Euclid started with many axioms about geometry. Then he used **deductive reasoning** and logic to come to hundreds of new conclusions about geometry.

Geometry is important in many of today's professions. Architects must understand geometry to design buildings. Airplane and spaceship pilots use geometry to plot their courses. Artists, **engineers,** and designers also use many ideas from geometry.

Architects and builders must use geometry to design and build structures.

► Prime Numbers

Prime numbers, such as the ones shown above, have long fascinated mathematicians.

The Greek mathematician Euclid made many important contributions to mathematics in the 300's B.C. In his textbook *Elements*, he discussed many ideas about **prime numbers.**

A prime number is a whole number that can only be divided evenly by itself and one. For example, the number 7 is a prime number, because you cannot divide 7 by any other numbers—except 1—without getting a remainder (a number left

over). On the other hand, the number 9 is not a prime number. You can divide 9 by 3 without getting a remainder. The ten smallest prime numbers are 2, 3, 5, 7, 11, 13, 17, 19, 23, and 29.

The number 2 is the only even prime number. It only divides by itself and 1. But all other prime numbers are odd, not even. This is because all even numbers divide by 2 without a remainder.

Euclid proved that there is an endless amount of prime numbers. He also proved an interesting and important feature of prime numbers. He showed that you can get any whole number simply by multiplying prime numbers together. For example, you can get the number 30 by multiplying the following prime numbers to-

FUN FACT

In 2008, mathematicians in the United States discovered a prime number that is 13 million **digits** long!

gether: 2 x 3 x 5. This is true for all whole numbers. This idea shows that prime numbers are like building blocks for other whole numbers.

Many mathematicians after Euclid's time were fascinated with prime numbers. In the 200's B.C., a Greek mathematician named Eratosthenes (*ehr uh TOS thuh neez*) devised a method to figure out if a number is prime or not. His method is called the Sieve (*sihv*) of Eratosthenes. People used this method for hundreds of years. Today, computers are a much faster tool for finding prime numbers than the Sieve of Eratosthenes.

Knowing prime numbers can make it easier to solve some math problems, but there are not too many practical uses for them. However, they are used to make codes that are very difficult to break.

A prime number can only be divided evenly by itself and one. Some prime numbers are shown in red below.

Euclid developed many important ideas in mathematics.

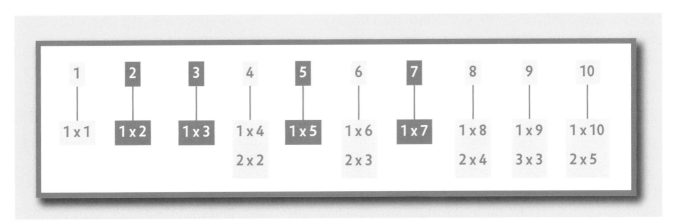

1	2	3	4	5	6	7	8	9	10
1 x 1	1 x 2	1 x 3	1 x 4	1 x 5	1 x 6	1 x 7	1 x 8	1 x 9	1 x 10
			2 x 2		2 x 3		2 x 4	3 x 3	2 x 5

The Value of Pi

Circles have several important mathematical qualities.

Circles have long fascinated mathematicians. As ancient mathematicians studied circles, they discovered a relationship between a circle's **circumference** and **diameter.**

The circumference is the length of the curved line of the circle. For example, if you measured the length around the edge of a pizza, you would be measuring its circumference. A circle's diameter is the length of a line drawn straight through its center. If you put a ruler across the center of a pizza and measured it from crust to crust, you would be measuring its diameter.

For thousands of years, mathematicians have known that the relationship between a circle's circumference and diameter is important. The number you get when you divide a circle's circumference by its diameter is called **pi.** Pi is also sometimes written as the Greek **symbol,** π.

The number pi is the same for all circles, no matter how big or small they are. The number pi has many uses in physics (the study of matter and energy) and **engineering,** so it is an important number to know. But the exact number pi is not easy to calculate (figure out). The ancient Chinese used the number 3, since it is somewhat close to the **value** of pi.

In the 200's B.C., the Greek

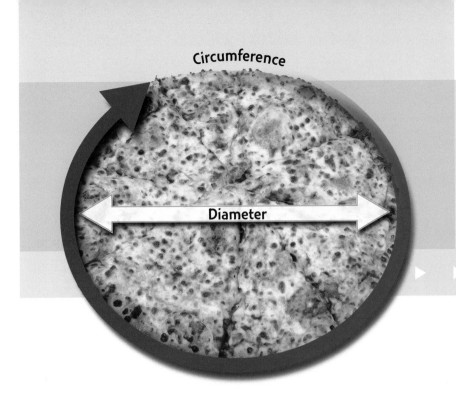

Circumference

Diameter

Pi is the number you get when you divide a circle's circumference by its diameter.

mathematician Archimedes (*AHR kuh MEE deez*) figured out a fairly accurate measurement of pi. He showed that the value of pi is close to the number 3.14.

In the A.D. 100's, the astronomer Ptolemy (*TOL uh mee*) came up with an even more accurate value for pi. His value for pi was 3.1416. But pi is not exactly equal to 3.1416.

Today, computers can estimate the number pi to trillions of **decimal places.** However, there is no exact value for pi that we can write with our numbers. This is because it cannot be written as a **fraction** or with a limited number of decimal places.

Archimedes was a Greek mathematician who figured out a fairly accurate measurement for pi.

► Algebra

From the beginning of **civilization,** mathematics has helped people to solve problems. Tools like the **abacus** made it easier for people to buy and sell goods. The study of **geometry** helped people measure land and plan buildings. But complex math problems required a new way of solving them, called **algebra.**

Algebra helps people find answers to mathematical problems that cannot be solved just with **arithmetic** (adding, subtracting, multiplying, and dividing). Algebra uses letters to stand for unknown numbers in problems.

In algebra, letters are used to represent unknown numbers.

Al-Khwarizmi

Al-Khwarizmi (780?-850?) was an Arab mathematician of the Islamic empire. He did much of his writing and research in Baghdad, in what is now Iraq. He wrote a book that introduced a system of numbering that was used in India. This system later spread to Europe, and we use a version of it today. Translations of al-Khwarizmi's works helped spread mathematical knowledge from India and the Middle East into Europe.

For example, let's say a boy named Euclid wanted to figure out how much his dog weighs, but the dog will not stay still on the scale. Euclid knows his own weight is 120 pounds. If Euclid holds the dog in his arms and stands on a scale, the scale reads 140 pounds.

Using algebra, we can figure out how much Euclid's dog weighs. Let the letter x stand for the dog's unknown weight. We know that Euclid's weight (120), plus the weight of the dog (x), equals 140. So we can write the following **equation:**

$$120 + x = 140$$

What could x be? The only number that works in the equation is 20. So we know that Euclid's dog must weigh 20 pounds.

In some algebra problems, only one number works for x. In other problems, many numbers might work for x. More complicated algebra problems use several letters for unknown numbers.

The ancient Egyptians used simple algebra. The ancient Babylonians, Greeks, Chinese, and the Hindus in India added to the understanding of algebra over hundreds of years. The Arabs also greatly advanced algebra. The word *algebra* comes from the title of a book by an Arab mathematician named al-Khwarizmi (*al KWAHR*

Algebra has many practical uses. You can even use it to figure out how much a pet weighs.

ihz mee), written in the A.D. 800's. The original Arabic word, *al-jabr*, means "restoration" or "completion."

Algebra is important to many professions. **Engineers** and scientists use algebra every day. Businesses rely on algebra to solve many problems. Because of its importance in modern living, algebra is studied in schools and colleges in all parts of the world. Today, computers can quickly solve many algebra problems.

► The Concept of Zero

The concept of zero helped these Italian bankers of long ago keep track of their accounts.

The words for numbers have not always existed. Ancient people counted using small objects, like pebbles or markings on wood. These objects or markings were **symbols** for certain numbers. The invention of the **abacus** helped people count and arrange these numbers.

The earliest words for numbers were based on the numbers' symbols. For example, some ancient people used a hand symbol for the number 5, so their word for "5" was the same as their word for "hand." Eventually, people began counting with these words. However, ancient people did not have a word or a

symbol for the number zero.

It is hard to imagine counting numbers without the number zero. But zero is actually a tricky idea. After all, most symbols stand for something—but zero stands for nothing. Today, we use 0 as a **digit.** Digits are the symbols 0, 1, 2, 3, 4, 5, 6, 7, 8, and 9. We combine these digits to make many larger numbers.

There is evidence that the Maya of Central America were using symbols for zero by about A.D. 250. Several hundred years later and across the globe, Hindu mathematicians in India developed a symbol for zero, around the A.D. 800's. They called

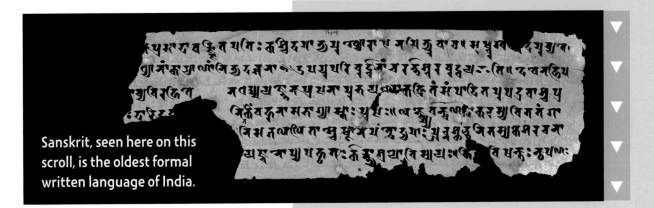

Sanskrit, seen here on this scroll, is the oldest formal written language of India.

this symbol *sunya*, which meant "void" or "empty" in Sanksrit, a language of India. They used this symbol as a digit, just as we do today with 0.

The *sunya* symbol spread from India to Arab lands. By the late 1400's, Europeans were using it. The English word *zero* is probably based on translations from the Sanskrit word *sunya*.

The concept of zero was an important breakthrough in mathematics. It would lead to the development of the **decimal system,** which is still used throughout the world.

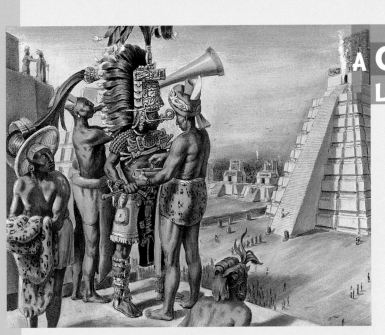

A **CLOSER** LOOK

The Maya of Central America are believed to be the first people to invent the number zero. They also created a number system that was based on 20's, 200's, 2,000's, and so on. The Maya system worked just as well as our decimal system does today.

The Maya made great advances in astronomy and mathematics and developed an accurate yearly calendar. They also produced remarkable architecture, painting, pottery, and sculpture.

```
                    TE#     TR#
         OP#  005749801035    3.38
ST#          007065200750    2.97
             007065200750    2.97
             006025835503   14.96
             0681131763 69    4.97
             002340035457    0.93
             005963148202    3.87
             002340035458    0.93
             005920000731    0.93
                 SUBTOTAL   35.91
             HST 15%         4.88
                   TOTAL    40.79
             DEBIT  TEND    40.79
             CHANGE DUE      0.00
                   RT
GST/HST


PURCHASE TRANSACTION RECORD
     40.79
CHEQUING       ***********
RRN # :
AUTH #:
00 APPROVED-THANK YOU
TERMINAL ID:
```

The numbers we write today are based on the decimal system.

Ancient people all wrote numbers differently, but they had similar number systems. In most early number systems, people wrote a number as a list of basic **symbols.** However, they had to add all the symbols together to get the actual number. For example, using **Roman numerals,** the number 15 would be written as the symbol for ten (X) and the symbol for five (V): XV. The Egyptians, Greeks, and Romans all used this kind of system.

Mathematicians in India faced a similar problem. They had symbols for the numbers 1 through 9. They also had words for "tens," "hundreds," and so on. But they did not have a symbol for zero until the A.D. 800's. If they wanted to write the number 250, they had to write out "2 hundreds, 5 tens." There was no easy way for them to show the number has "no ones." The invention of the zero solved this problem. It allowed them to develop the **decimal system,** the number system we still use today.

$$\underset{\text{Hundreds}}{2} \quad \underset{\text{Tens}}{5} \quad \underset{\text{Ones}}{0} \quad \underset{\text{Decimal}}{.} \quad \underset{\text{Tenths}}{0}$$

A decimal point allows people to write number places smaller than one.

The decimal system is a way of writing numbers. Any number, from huge quantities to tiny **fractions,** can be written in the decimal system using only 10 basic symbols: 1, 2, 3, 4, 5, 6, 7, 8, 9, and 0. The **value** of any of these symbols depends on the place it occupies in the number. For example, the symbol 2 has different values in the numbers 25 and 502, because the 2 is in a different place in each of the numbers.

As with the symbol for zero, the decimal system spread from India to nearby Arab lands. It eventually

reached Europe in the early 1200's. By the mid-1400's, schools and universities in many countries began teaching the decimal system.

The decimal system had many advantages over Roman numerals, which most people in Europe used at the time. Because it was now simple to write large numbers, people could perform calculations using just a pen and paper. It also takes less space to write a number in the decimal system. Larger numbers can be written without new symbols.

F U N   F A C T

The word *decimal* comes from *decem,* the Latin word for "ten."

Decimal Numeral	Roman Numeral
1	I
2	II
3	III
4	IIII or IV
5	V
6	VI
7	VII
8	VIII
9	VIIII or IX
10	X

Many decimal numerals are simpler to write and take less space than Roman numerals.

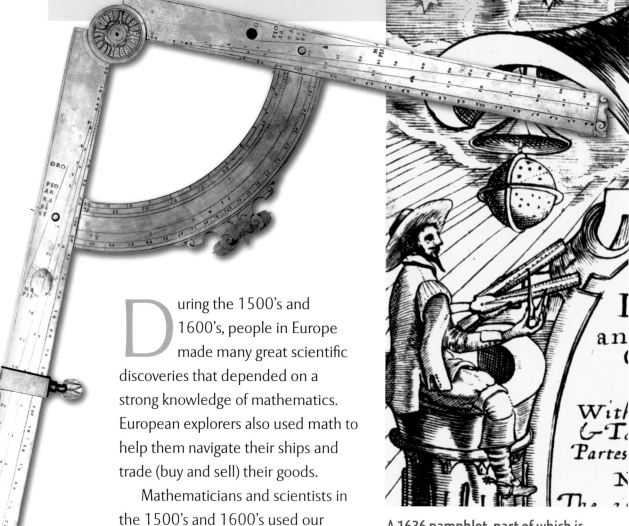

During the 1500's and 1600's, people in Europe made many great scientific discoveries that depended on a strong knowledge of mathematics. European explorers also used math to help them navigate their ships and trade (buy and sell) their goods.

Mathematicians and scientists in the 1500's and 1600's used our modern **decimal system** to make calculations. However, they had to figure out complicated math problems by hand, which took much time and effort. To save time, mathematicians developed a number of important tools and techniques that helped them work out math problems and take measurements.

The sector was an important tool that helped people make measurements quickly and accurately.

A 1636 pamphlet, part of which is shown above, showed sailors how to use the sector to navigate their ships.

One such tool was the **sector,** which was invented by the Italian scientist Galileo (*GAL uh LAY oh*) in 1597. The sector helped people take detailed measurements.

The sector looked like two rulers

joined together with a hinge on one end, allowing the tool to open and close like a mouth. It contained several different **scales**—that is, a series of marks that are equal distances apart. Each scale could be used to solve a different type of mathematical problem.

People used the sector to measure the height of distant objects, such as mountains. They also used it to solve **geometry,** multiplication, and division problems.

Galileo based the sector's design on an earlier tool called the gunner's compass, which helped soldiers fire a cannonball more accurately. A can-nonball follows a curved path through the air, making it difficult to judge where it will land. The gunner's compass measured the elevation of the cannon's barrel, which helped soldiers estimate the path that the cannonball would take. Galileo improved the gunner's compass by adding several mathematical scales to its legs.

Today, people use computers and modern **calculators** to solve many types of mathematical problems that were once solved with the sector.

Galileo

Galileo Galilei (1564-1642) was an Italian scientist and mathematician. He designed several important devices for making scientific measurements. These included the sector and a device for weighing objects in water. Galileo also improved the design of the telescope.

Galileo helped pave the way for modern science. He supported a theory proposed by astronomer Nicolaus Copernicus, which stated that Earth moves around the sun. At the time, most people believed Earth stood still, and that the sun moved around Earth. The Roman Catholic Church punished Galileo because they thought his ideas went against the Bible. Galileo was not allowed to leave his house for the rest of his life.

▶ Calculators

By the 1600's, mathematicians had developed special tables (arrangements of numbers in columns or rows) that helped them solve certain types of math problems more quickly. But many problems still took a long time to solve, since their solutions had to be written out by hand.

In the 1620's, an English mathematician named William Oughtred invented a new kind of calculating device. His invention, called the **slide rule,** looked like a ruler with pieces that could slide up and down its

Blaise Pascal invented this calculating machine in the 1600's. It used wheels and gears to solve math problems.

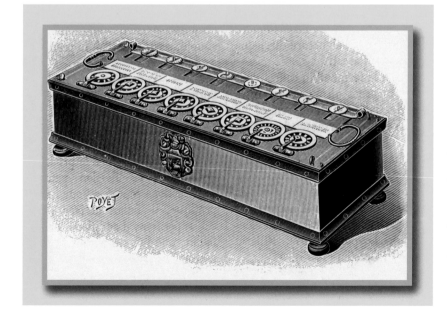

length. The sliding pieces, along with the ruler, had many kinds of markings and numbers. By lining up the sliding pieces with markings on the ruler, a person could quickly find the answers to multiplication and division problems. Mathematicians could also use slide rules to solve more complicated problems. Scientists and **engineers** used slide rules for hundreds of years.

The slide rule was not the only calculating device invented in the 1600's. Others were machines with several **gears,** which turned wheels that had numbers written on them. By turning one wheel, the gears moved the other wheels. A person could compare the numbers on the wheels to quickly do addition and subtraction. Some machines could also do multiplication or division problems.

Calculating machines were not as

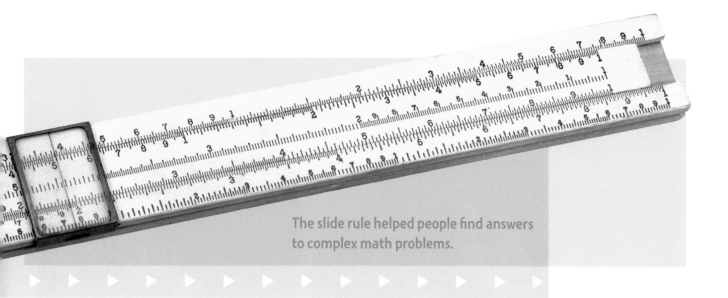

The slide rule helped people find answers to complex math problems.

widely used as slide rules, but they helped pave the way for many important inventions. Many ideas behind modern computers come from the calculating machines of the 1600's.

In the 1960's, scientists developed the **electronic calculator,** which made solving problems faster and easier than ever. Electronic calculators use miniature circuits (paths followed by an **electric current**) to perform calculations automatically.

At first, calculators could be used only to solve simple **arithmetic.** Over time, however, calculators have become more powerful. Today, they can be used to solve complex mathematical problems.

Modern electronic calculators can solve many kinds of math problems.

F U N F A C T The counting board and the **abacus** were the first kinds of calculating devices.

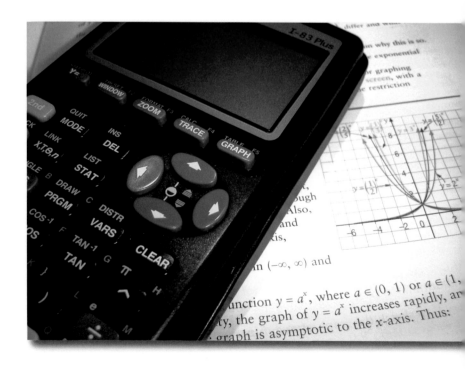

▶ Probability Theory

People can use probability theory to predict outcomes, such as the chance that a coin will land on heads or tails (right) or the chance that dice will land on a certain number (left).

What are the chances that a tossed coin will land on the tails side? If you throw a 6-sided die, what are the chances that it will land on 6? **Probability theory** is a kind of mathematics that answers such questions.

People have long been interested in games of chance. Probability theory is a way of writing and thinking about games of chance with math. For example, there are two sides to a coin. So the chances of a coin ending up on one of the sides can be written as a **fraction:** $^1/_2$. Similarly, the chances of landing on any one side of a 6-sided die can be written as $^1/_6$.

Two people developed probability theory in the 1600's. They were Pierre de Fermat (*fehr MAH*), a French mathematician, and Blaise Pascal (*blehz pas KAL*), a Swiss mathematician, philosopher, and scientist.

Pascal and Fermat wrote letters to each other about games of chance. Pascal also invented a pattern of numbers called Pascal's triangle. (See the "Closer Look" sidebar on this page.) In Pascal's triangle, numbers are arranged in rows. Adding numbers together on higher rows gives the numbers on the lower rows. Pascal's triangle helps figure out probabilities. Later mathematicians and scientists also added to probability theory.

With probability theory, people can make useful predictions (educated guesses) based on known information. It allows people to think about data—facts, figures, and information—with mathematical exactness. People have collected data since ancient times. For example, the Bible tells stories about surveys that counted the number of people living in an area. During the **Middle Ages** (A.D. 400's through the 1400's), government and church leaders collected data about people and their property.

Today, the science of collecting and thinking about such data is called **statistics.** It is based on probability theory. Doctors, scientists, and politicians all use statistics in their work.

In Pascal's triangle, each number is the sum of the two numbers on the row directly above it.

A CLOSER LOOK

Pascal's triangle is easy to make. Start out with the top two rows. To get numbers in the lower rows, simply add numbers together that are side by side.

Pascal's triangle has no bottom—it can go down as far as you wish. It has many interesting number patterns. Look at the triangle at the bottom of this page. How many patterns of numbers do you see?

Blaise Pascal

													1													
												1		1												
											1		2		1											
										1		3		3		1										
									1		4		6		4		1									
								1		5		10		10		5		1								
							1		6		15		20		15		6		1							
						1		7		21		35		35		21		7		1						
					1		8		28		56		70		56		28		8		1					
				1		9		36		84		126		126		84		36		9		1				
			1		10		45		120		210		252		210		120		45		10		1			
		1		11		55		165		330		462		462		330		165		55		11		1		
	1		12		66		220		495		792		924		792		495		220		66		12		1	
1		13		78		286		715		1287		1716		1716		1287		715		286		78		13		1
1	14		91		364		1001		2002		3003		3432		3003		2002		1001		364		91		14	1

The Binary Number System

The binary number system uses only two digits—1 and 0.

Throughout history, people have used several kinds of number systems. A number system is how we write and think about numbers. Today, people use the **decimal system.** It features 10 **digits**—0, 1, 2, 3, 4, 5, 6, 7, 8, and 9. With these 10 digits, we can write many kinds of numbers. The Maya of Central America used a number system based on 20 digits. Other systems are based on the number 12. For example, there are 12 inches in a foot.

During the 1600's, a German mathematician and philosopher named Gottfried Wilhelm Leibniz (*GOHT freet VIHL helm LYP nihts*) invented an important new number system called the **binary number system.** The binary system is based on 2. It only has two digits—1 and 0. Leibniz figured out a way to write all kinds of numbers with just these two digits.

For many years, people ignored Leibniz's binary system. Mathematicians were already used to the decimal system. And binary was hard for people to learn and use.

The most important use of the

Gottfried Wilhelm Liebniz invented the binary number system.

binary system began in the 1940's, when people first developed computers. Electric power runs through a computer's **circuits,** the paths over which an **electric current** flows. Just like digits in the binary system, this electric power comes only in two forms—charged or uncharged. In computers, each charge is called a **bit.** The word *bit* means binary digit. A bit can either be 1 or 0.

Computers use binary numbers as a kind of language. A binary number can stand for all sorts of things—decimal numbers, letters, and even pictures and sounds. Without the binary system, computers as we know them today would not exist.

Computers use binary numbers as a kind of language.

▶ Calculus

Calculus deals with curved shapes, such as the arc of this roller coaster.

Even the earliest mathematicians dealt with shapes and their **areas.** Figuring out a shape's area is an important part of **geometry.** A rectangle's area is easy to find. It is equal to the rectangle's width, multiplied by its height. A cir-

cle's area is also easy to figure out. It is equal to half the circle's **diameter,** multiplied by itself, then multiplied by the number **pi**.

Many shapes are made out of rectangles, triangles, and circles. And mathematicians have long known how to find their areas. But how do you find the area of a curved shape that is not a circle? Finding such areas is much more complicated. **Calculus** is a kind of mathematics that deals with finding areas of curved shapes.

A Greek mathematician named Archimedes used a simple kind of calculus in the 200's B.C. But modern calculus wasn't invented until the 1600's. Two famous scientists invented modern calculus at nearly the same time. One of them was the English scientist, Sir Isaac Newton. The other was the German philosopher and mathematician, Gottfried Wilhelm Leibniz (*GOHT freet VIHL helm LYP nihts*).

Calculus does more than help people figure out the areas of curved shapes. Another way to think about calculus is that it helps to measure

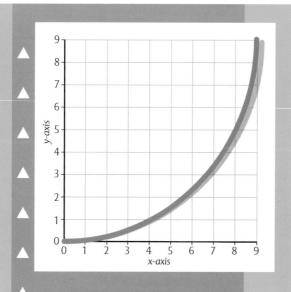

Calculus helps measure changing values, such as the height of this red line.

Sir Isaac Newton

Sir Isaac Newton (1642-1727) was an English scientist, astronomer, and mathematician. He used mathematics to show how the universe is held together with gravity. In 1687, he published a book called *Mathematical Principles of Natural Philosophy*. In this book, Newton showed exactly how gravity worked, using the language of mathematics.

In addition to his many contributions to science, Newton is famous for his invention of calculus. He invented modern calculus at the same time as another famous mathematician named Gottfried Wilhelm Leibniz.

Engineers must use calculus to design airplane parts.

change. This is because a curve is basically a line that changes its height. Steep curves change quickly. Shallow curves, on the other hand, change slowly. In order to measure the area under a curve, you have to figure out how fast or slow the curve is changing. And in order to do that, you need to use techniques in calculus.

Calculus has many important uses. **Engineers** use calculus to design the curved shapes of automobiles and airplanes. People also use calculus to measure changing speeds, from shooting bullets to soaring rockets. Many complicated math problems can only be solved with calculus.

The metric system allowed people from many places to use the same kind of measurements.

During the late 1600's and 1700's, Europeans used reasoning and science more and more. This period in history is called the **Enlightenment.** During this time, scientists from different countries worked together. Trade (buying and selling goods) also increased between countries. Both traders and scientists used advanced mathematical ideas and tools.

However, people from different countries had different ways of measuring. They used different **scales** to weigh materials and to measure their lengths. Even in a single country, there were often many different ways of measuring. Without a single, commonly accepted way of measuring, it was difficult for traders to do business. Scientists had trouble comparing their measurements.

In 1790, the French government asked French scientists to make a measuring system that could be used throughout the world. The next year, scientists worked out the **metric system.** This system is based on a single length of measurement, called the **meter.** The meter was defined as the distance from the North Pole to the equator, divided by 10 million.

The metric system was better than other measuring systems in several ways. In the metric system, each type of measurement has a single "family" of **units.** For example, length is measured in centimeters, meters, and kilometers. Weight is measured in grams, centigrams, and kilograms.

Each member of the "family" is bigger or smaller than other members based on the **decimal system.** For example, centimeters, meters, and kilo-

Metric conversion table

What you know	Multiply by	To find
Length and distance		
inches (in)	2.54	centimeters
feet (ft)	30.48	centimeters
yards	0.9144	meters
miles (mi)	1.609	kilometers
Volume (liquid)		
fluid ounces	29.57	milliliters
pints (U.S.)	0.4732	liters
Weight and mass		
ounces (oz)	28.350	grams
pounds (lb)	0.4536	kilograms
Temperatures	$\frac{5}{9}$ (after	
°Fahrenheit (°F)	subtracting 32	°Celsius (°C)

This table shows how to convert some common measurements into metric units.

meters are all related to each other based on the number 10. A centimeter is 100 times smaller than a meter. A kilometer is 1,000 times bigger than a meter. Using measurements based on 10's is much simpler than using measurements based on other numbers.

In 1875, 17 countries signed the Treaty of the Meter, which made the metric system official in those countries. By 1960, most developed countries had adopted the metric system.

Nearly all scientists use the metric system today. Some countries—including the United States—do not officially use the metric system. But many scientists and **engineers** in the United States use it.

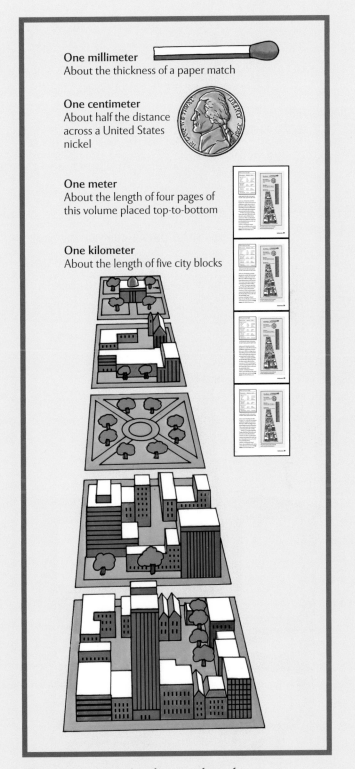

One millimeter
About the thickness of a paper match

One centimeter
About half the distance across a United States nickel

One meter
About the length of four pages of this volume placed top-to-bottom

One kilometer
About the length of five city blocks

The metric system's values are based on 10's, using the decimal system.

The 1800's were filled with discoveries in science and mathematics. As scientific and mathematic knowledge grew, people invented better calculating tools. Today's computers all come from these ideas and inventions.

One such invention came from a French weaver named Joseph Marie Jacquard. In 1801, Jacquard invented a loom that used punched cards, which controlled the weaving needles. The punched-out holes let the needles pass through. Areas without holes blocked the needles. By punching out certain patterns of holes, the cards could be "programmed" to weave certain designs over and over.

An English mathematician named Charles Babbage was inspired by Jacquard's idea. In the 1820's, he used a similar idea to develop a new kind of calculating machine. Babbage's invention was supposed to do complex mathematical problems based on a series of instructions.

These instructions were prepared like Jacquard's punch cards. But instead of using the cards to weave a cloth pattern, Babbage's machine used the cards to do complex calculations. The cards were fed into the machine, which was powered by steam. Depending on the card pattern, the machine would add, subtract, multiply, or divide, and print out a result. It would also do much

The punched-card-controlled sewing machine was a forerunner to complex calculating machines.

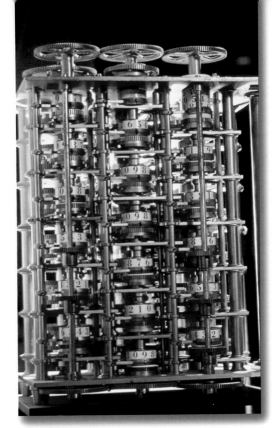

Charles Babbage's machine could perform complex calculations using patterns on punched cards.

more complicated math problems.

Babbage worked on his invention for nearly 50 years. He died before he finished it. But many of his ideas are used in modern computers today. For example, each place in the card either had one hole or no holes, and so the pattern of holes could work as **binary digits.** Modern computers use binary digits as **bits.** Babbage's machine also stored the punch cards and reused them in complicated calculations. This is similar to how modern computers use memory.

Since Babbage's invention, computer technology has changed dramat-

F
U
N

F
A
C
T

Babbage never finished his analytical engine. But in 1991, the Science Museum in London built a working version of it.

ically. The first **electronic** computer was invented in 1939 by John V. Atanasoff, an American mathematician and physicist, and Clifford Berry, an American graduate student in electrical **engineering**. By the 1950's, new technologies allowed computers to get smaller and more powerful.

Personal computers, or the computers found in homes, schools, and offices, didn't become widely used until the 1980's. Today, it is impossible to imagine a world without computers. Together with the **Internet,** they have rapidly sped the process of sending and receiving information from all parts of the world.

In 1977, Stephen G. Wozniak (left) and Steven P. Jobs introduced the Apple II, the first computer that was affordable to families, schools, and small businesses.

► Chaos Theory

People use chaos theory to help predict complex weather patterns.

During the late 1900's, mathematicians developed a new kind of math called **chaos theory,** which deals with complex, hard-to-predict systems. A theory is an explanation for something based on thought. Chaos theorists study how tiny changes affect huge, complicated systems.

With chaos theory, mathematicians start with complex forms and try to figure out the simple patterns behind them. A chaotic system is something that seems without pattern or plan, but isn't. The weather, the stock market, and the movement of billiard balls shooting across a pool table are examples of chaotic systems.

Let's look at the example of billiard balls to see how chaotic systems work. When you aim a billiard ball into a group of balls, the balls may move in ways that seem random. However, the directions in which they move depend entirely on how straight you shoot the first ball. If your aim is just a tiny bit off, the first ball may seem to shoot straight, but the next ball will be less straight.

FUN FACT

One popular way of thinking about chaos theory is called the "butterfly effect." According to chaos theory, a butterfly flapping its wings in a certain way can eventually affect huge weather patterns, like tornadoes.

The ball after that will be even less straight, and so on. Your original shot gets magnified over and over again as the system moves and changes.

What chaotic systems may do is difficult to predict. People can now use computers to make models of chaotic systems—that is, show how chaotic systems may behave. These models help mathematicians and scientists make predictions.

Chaos theory has helped make weather reports more accurate. It also helps scientists in many different fields think about their work.

The way billiard balls move across a table is an example of a chaotic system.

Benoit Mandelbrot

Benoit Mandelbrot (1924-) is a Polish-born mathematician. He and his family moved to France when he was 12 years old to escape the persecution of the Jews. He studied in France, and eventually moved to the United States.

Mandelbrot's studies in the 1960's helped pave the way to the development of chaos theory. Mandelbrot also did important work in a special field of **geometry**. Mandelbrot currently teaches mathematical sciences at Yale University in the United States.

Important Dates in Mathematics

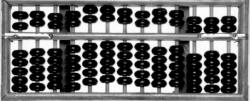

c. 3000 B.C. Ancient Egyptians developed a simple number system.

c. 3000 B.C. Ancient Egyptians developed the 3-4-5 triangle.

c. 2100 B.C. Ancient Babylonians developed a number system based on groups of 60.

c. 400 B.C. Ancient Greeks developed the Pythagorean theorem.

c. 300 B.C. The Greek mathematician Euclid created a mathematical textbook called *Elements*.

c. 300 B.C. The Greek mathematician Archimedes came up with the number 3.14 for pi.

c. 200 B.C. The method for identifying prime numbers was developed.

A.D. 200's Ancient people first used symbols to represent unknown numbers (algebra).

c. A.D. 250 The Maya in Central America invented a symbol for zero.

A.D. 595 Mathematicians in India developed the decimal system.

A.D. 800's The Persian mathematician Al-Khwarizmi wrote an influential book that included information on the decimal system.

Late A.D. 800's Mathematicians in India invented a symbol for zero.

Mid-1400's The decimal system spread throughout Europe.

Late 1500's The sector was invented.

1620's The slide rule was invented.

1640's The first calculating machine was invented.

1654 Probability theory was invented.

Late 1600's The binary number system was invented.

Late 1600's Calculus was invented.

1790 The metric system was first developed.

1801 The automated Jacquard loom was invented.

1820's The first design of the mechanical computer was developed.

1960's The first electronic calculators were developed.

1960 The metric system was named the International System of Units.

1960's Chaos theory was developed.

Glossary

abacus a square or rectangular frame holding a row of wires or narrow wooden rods which are strung with beads, used as a counting device.

algebra a field of mathematics that uses letters, such as x and y, to represent unknown numbers to solve problems.

angle the space between two lines or surfaces that meet.

area an amount of surface.

arithmetic the art or practice of computing or calculating by means of numbers.

axiom a mathematical statement that is assumed to be true.

binary number system a numbering system that uses only two digits (0 and 1) and groups numbers by twos and powers of two.

bit the basic unit of information in a digital computing system. Bits are expressed in binary notation so as to specify a choice between two possibilities, such as yes or no or off or on.

calculator a mechanical device that can perform many different mathematical operations quickly and accurately.

calculus a field of mathematics that deals with changing quantities.

chaos theory the study of how tiny changes affect complex systems.

circuit the complete path, or a part of it, over which an electric current flows.

circumference the distance around the outside of a circle.

civilization nations and peoples that have reached advanced stages in social development.

cubit an ancient measure of length.

decimal place the position of a digit to the right of a decimal point.

decimal system a system of counting that puts objects in groups of ten.

deductive reasoning a type of reasoning that begins with statements known to be true and combines them in a logical way to reach a conclusion.

degree a unit for measuring the opening of an angle or an arc of a circle or a unit for measuring temperature.

denominator the number below the line in a fraction, which shows the size of the parts in their relation to the whole.

diameter the distance across the center of the circle.

digit any of the figures 0, 1, 2, 3, 4, 5, 6, 7, 8, or 9.

electric current the movement or flow of electric charges.

electronic of or having to do with electrons.

engineer; engineering a person who invents, plans, or builds things, such as engines, machines, bridges, or buildings; the use of science to design structures, machines, and products.

Enlightenment the period during the late 1600's and 1700's when people began to rely more on the use of reason to solve problems, also called the Age of Reason.

equation a statement of equality between two quantities, indicated by using the equal sign (=) between them.

fraction one or more of the equal parts of a whole number.

gear a wheel having teeth that fit into the teeth of another wheel to move it or be moved by it.

geometry a branch of mathematics that involves the study of the shape, size, and positions of lines, angles, curves, and figures.

Internet a vast network of computers that connects many of the world's businesses, institutions, and individuals.

meter a unit of measurement equal to one ten-millionth of the distance from the North Pole to the equator; the primary unit of distance measurement used in the metric system.

metric system a system of measurements based on the meter.

Middle Ages the period in European history between ancient and modern times, from about the A.D. 400's through the 1400's.

numeral a figure, letter, or word standing for a number.

numerator the number above the line in a fraction, which shows how many parts are taken.

personal computer a computer used by one person at a time.

pi the relation between the circumference of a circle and its diameter, also written as the Greek symbol π.

prime number a whole number other than one, such as two, five, and seven, that can be divided without a remainder only by itself and one.

probability theory a branch of mathematics that deals with the chances of different possible outcomes of random events.

Pythagorean theorem the statement that, in a right triangle, the sum of the square of the length of the hypotenuse equals the sum of the squares of the lengths of the other two sides.

right angle an angle that is formed by a line perpendicular to another line; angle of 90 degrees.

Roman of or having to do with ancient Rome or its people. The Roman Empire controlled most of Europe and the Middle East from 27 B.C. to A.D. 476.

scale a series of marks made along a line or curve at regular distances to use in measuring.

sector an instrument also known as a proportional compass, made up of two rulers marked with a number of different measuring scales, connected by a hinge at one end.

slide rule a calculating tool that has sliding rulers marked with different scales that can be used to estimate quickly the solutions to complicated mathematical calculations.

statistics a field of mathematics that deals with collecting and analyzing data.

symbol something that represents an object or idea.

table an arrangement of numbers in columns or rows.

unit an amount used to describe other measurements of the same kind.

value the number or amount represented by a symbol.

▶ Additional Resources

Books:

- *Amazing Leonardo da Vinci Inventions You Can Build Yourself* by Maxine Anderson (Nomad Press VT, 2006).

- *Great Inventions: The Illustrated Science Encyclopedia* by Peter Harrison, Chris Oxlade, and Stephen Bennington (Southwater Publishing, 2001).

- *Great Inventions of the 20th Century* by Peter Jedicke (Chelsea House Publications, 2007).

- *So You Want to Be an Inventor?* by Judith St. George (Philomel Books, 2002).

- *What a Great Idea! Inventions that Changed the World* by Stephen M. Tomecek (Scholastic, 2003).

Web Sites:

- Ask Dr. Math
  http://www.forum.swarthmore.edu/dr.math
  Question and answer service from Swarthmore College in Swarthmore, Pennsylvania, for students and teachers of mathematics.

- Geometry Problem of the Week
  http://forum.swarthmore.edu/geopow
  A collection of practice problems in geometry hosted by the Math Forum, an online educational network based in Swarthmore, Pennsylvania.

- The MacTutor History of Mathematics Archive
  http://www-groups.dcs.st-and.ac.uk/~history
  Articles about the history of mathematics from the University of St. Andrews in St. Andrews, Scotland.

- Mathematics Glossary - Middle Years
  http://MathCentral.uregina.ca/RR/glossary/middle

A glossary of mathematics terms from the Saskatchewan Math Teachers' Society, headquartered in Saskatoon, Saskatchewan.

- Mathematicians of the African Diaspora
  http://www.math.buffalo.edu/mad/Ancient-Africa/index.html
  History of mathematics in ancient Africa, from the mathematics department of the State University of New York at Buffalo.

- Mathematics (Rome Reborn: The Vatican Library & Renaissance Culture)
  http://lcweb.loc.gov/exhibits/vatican/math.html
  The history of mathematics from the U.S. Library of Congress.

- NRICH Online Maths Club
  http://nrich.maths.org
  Online mathematics club from Cambridge University in Cambridge, England, featuring puzzles and games as well as information about history, careers, and practical applications of mathematics.

- Science U: The Geometry Center
  http://www.ScienceU.com/geometry
  A commercial site that provides interactive geometry games and puzzles developed by Geometry Technologies, Inc., in St. Paul, Minnesota.

- This is MEGA Mathematics!
  http://www.c3.lanl.gov/mega-math
  Mathematics learning activities from Los Alamos National Laboratory in Los Alamos, New Mexico.

▶ Index

A
abacus, 6-7, 24, 31
Africa, 7
algebra, 22-23
al-Khwarizmi, 22, 23
angle, 14-15
Arabs, 11, 25, 27; algebra, 22, 23
Archimedes, 20-21, 36
area, 15, 36
arithmetic, 22, 31
axiom, 17

B
Babbage, Charles, 40-41
Babylon, 6, 9, 10, 23
Bible, 33
billiard ball motion, 43
binary number system, 34-35, 41
bit, 35, 41
butterfly effect, 42

C
calculator, 11, 29-31. *See also* computer
calculus, 36-37
centimeter, 38-39
chance. *See* probability theory
chaos theory, 42
chaotic system, 42-43
China, 7, 20, 23
circle, 20-21
circumference, 20-21
compass, gunner's, 29
computer: electronic, 35, 41; mechanical, 40-41
cowrie, 7
cubit, 12, 13

D
decimal system, 11, 26-27, 34
denominator, 10-11
diameter, of circle, 20-21, 36
digit, 24, 34; binary, 41
distance. *See* length, unit of

E
Egypt, ancient, 16, 23, 26; counting system, 6; fractions, 10; length

measurements, 12; numerals, 8-9; Pythagorean theorem, 14
Elements (Euclid), 16-18
Enlightenment, 38
equation, 23
Eratosthenes, 19
Euclid, 16-19

F
Fermat, Pierre de, 32
fraction, 10-11, 27, 32

G
Galileo Galilei, 28-29
geometry, 16-17, 36
Greece, ancient, 9, 11, 23, 26; geometry, 16-17; pi, value of, 20-21; prime numbers, 18-19; Pythagorean theorem, 15

H
Hindu numeral system, 9

I
Inca, 7
India, 11, 24-27
Internet, 41
invention, 4

J
Jacquard, Joseph Marie, 40
Japan, ancient, 7
Jobs, Steven P., 41

K
kilometer, 38-39

L
Leibniz, Gottfried Wilhelm, 34-37
length, unit of, 12-13, 38-39
loom, of Jacquard, 40

M
Mandelbrot, Benoit, 43
mathematics, 4-5
Maya, 9, 24, 25, 34
meter, 38-39
Meter, Treaty of the, 39
metric system, 13, 38-39
Middle Ages, 33

N
Newton, Sir Isaac, 36, 37
number system, 34
numeral, 8-9
numerator, 10-11

O
Oughtred, William, 30

P
Pascal, Blaise, 30-33
Pascal's triangle, 33
personal computer, 41
pi, 20-21, 36
prime number, 18-19
probability theory, 32-33
Ptolemy, 21
Pyramids, of Egypt, 10, 12, 13
Pythagoras, 15
Pythagorean theorem, 14-15

R
right angle, 14-15
Roman numeral, 9, 26, 27
Rome, ancient, 9, 26

S
Sanskrit, 25
science, 4-5
sector, 28-29
shell, 16
Sieve of Eratosthenes, 19
slide rule, 30-31
snowflake, 16
square, area of, 15
statistics, 33
sunya, 24-25
symbol, 6, 8, 24, 26

T
triangle: Pascal's, 33; right, 14-15

U
unit, 12

W
weight, 38, 39
Wozniak, Stephen G., 41

Z
zero, concept of, 24-25